OUR CHILDREN ARE NOT ARE NOT PREPARED

A Teacher's Thoughts on Education

Dr. Pingnan Shi, Ph.D.

*First to my Lord, Jesus Chrsit. Without Him, my life
has no meaning nor purpose.*

*Second to my wife, Hui Peng, for her love and care
especially when I was at the rock bottom.*

*Third to my children, Allan and Allison Shi, for
giving me the reason to become a high school math
teacher.*

*Lastly to my friends and supporters
for believing in me.*

TABLE OF CONTENTS

OUR CHILDREN ARE NOT PREPARED FOR THEIR FUTURE

Is America's Education System Ruining Students?

"**A**merica's high schools are obsolete," Bill Gates made this startling remark at the 2005 National Education Summit on High Schools. To understand what he meant and the urgency with which he addressed his audience, let us look at what kind of jobs our children will have.

There are two kinds of jobs. The first one is the kind of jobs their future bosses do not want to do, so they are willing to hire someone. Examples are taking orders in a fast-food restaurant, making pizzas, mowing grass, or working on an assembly line. You are told what to do and how to do it. The median salary is less than $40K. This kind of jobs will be replaced by robots, industrial automation, and artificial intelligence. The essential skill required: following orders.

The second kind of jobs is such that their bosses cannot do, so they have to hire someone. Examples are engineering and technical jobs. Nobody tells you what to do and how to do it; you have to figure it out. The median salary is above $70K. This kind of jobs will grow as technology keeps advancing. The essential skill required: creative problem-solving.

After twelve years of public education, what will our children have learned? Most current high school graduates don't know how to use algebra; forget everything in geometry; are confused about trigonometry; have no clue about calculus. They cannot write persuasive essays; have no idea about logic fallacies; cannot think logically and critically. Many colleges are forced to provide remedial courses in Math and English because many incoming freshmen are not ready for college-level courses. The eight years of secondary education are totally wasted for most of high school graduates. If they are good students, the only skill they have learned in school is how to follow orders.

So the only kind of jobs they can do is the first one. But they face losing competition from robots and industrial automation. As warned by President Obama in this year's economic report, "What is true — and the reason that a lot of Americans feel anxious — is that the economy has been changing in profound ways, starting long before the Great Recession. Today, technology doesn't just replace jobs on the assembly line but rather affects any job where work can be automated. Companies in a global economy face tougher competition from abroad, and they can locate anywhere. As a result, workers have less leverage for a raise. And more and more wealth and income are concentrated at the very top."

Why?

Mr. Gates answered it in his speech: "Our high schools were designed fifty years ago to meet the needs of another age. Until we design them to meet the needs of the 21st century, we will keep limiting — even ruining — the lives of millions of Americans every year."

That age is when factories needed human labor to do assembly work. The workers only need to know how to follow orders. But with the rapid advancement of technology in the past twenty years, the Capital has found a much better workforce: robots. They are cheaper, more reliable, and more adaptive. The push for the $15 per hour minimum wage only accelerates the pace of replacing Humans with Machines. Watch a video on Tesla's Gigafactory, and you will see what is happening. Manufacturing companies may come back, but not with assembly-line jobs.

Our children are facing a much different future. They need creative problem-solving skills to become engineers who can design robots and technicians who can fix machines. Our education system needs a much-needed overhaul. But it won't happen unless parents get into the driver's seat. We cannot leave it to politicians and the teachers' unions.

HOW MATH
SET ME FREE

Seeking Truth Among Lies

I was trapped. I grew up in a small town in China during the Cultural Revolution. My dad was locked up in a makeshift prison because Chairman Mao overthrew the entire Communist Party leadership in a coup. My mom and we five kids were exiled to the countryside. Back then, the government told you where to live, where to go to school, where to work, and how much you are allowed to eat.

My town was a company town. The highest aspiration of my classmates and me was to work in that company because you could then live in a dorm and did not have to worry about going hungry. The company even had a clinic where you could get treated.

Almost all of the books published before the Cultural Revolution were banned and destroyed. But sometimes, you could still find an old book torn in the middle without the beginning and the ending chapters. Reading banned books was forbidden with punishment up to imprisonment. But things were relatively relaxed in small towns. In those books, I saw a totally different world. People have strange long names. They eat bread with jam. They drink milk instead of tea. They can eat as much as they want. They speak nicely to their children. They can go to universities that have millions of books, all kinds of books!

I wanted to go to that world. But my destiny was set. My mom told me that I could have her job when she retires. She expected me to get married and have a kid - we were only allowed to have one per couple and had to get permission from the government. She came from a much poorer background. Working in a factory was definitely a lot better than toiling in the field.

I did just OK in school, getting B's and C's. That was good enough for my parents. I didn't like Math. I did not understand it and didn't need it anyway. We boys just simply ganged together. Our parents were working and could not watch over us. We went swimming in the river and played games. I swam across the river after only four days of learning how to swim, and almost drowned during the process. After that, I was not afraid of water.

Many times we split into two groups and played war games. We started throwing mud at the kids on the other side. Eventually, our choice of weaponry escalated to rocks and slingshots until one or two boys got terribly injured. One of my classmates had one eye badly damaged. We would stay low for a while and start all over again in a month or two. Every summer, one or two boys we knew would drown in the river. We just got used to it.

One day, a colleague of my dad showed me a math problem, but he presented it as a puzzle. I loved solving puzzles. It took me a while to solve it but I asked for more. By solving math puzzles, I learned algebra, much like the same way I learned reading so I could read a torn up, yellow-colored, smelly old book.

My math grade improved. Pretty soon I was the undisputed number one in math in my entire grade. My teachers were shocked because they thought I was just a dumb kid. They treated me very nicely after they realized I had a talent. My other subjects started to improve as well. I won math competitions. It was nice to be treated like a celebrity.

Fortunately for me, before I got to high school, the Cultural Revolution was over. During the 10 years of that era, all the colleges in China were closed. Mao wanted to purge all Western influence from higher education. Now China was under a new leader, Deng Xiaoping, who wanted a different approach.

I was accepted to a college when I was 15 years old because I did well in the national college entrance exam. I didn't have to go. But I wanted to get out of my small town so badly and to see a different world as soon as I could.

I went to a college in Xian. It used to be China's capital for a thousand years until a thousand years ago. It became famous to the West for the Terra Cotta Warriors and the Silk Road. For the first time, I met classmates from different parts of China with different dialects. I saw my first snowfall which blanketed the whole campus. The most amazing thing is that I did not get frostbites for the first time. In the South, we did not have heating in schools. We kids always got frostbites in the winter. We thought that was just part of life.

I learned Calculus on my own because I suspected my teacher did not really understand it. I skipped so many Calculus classes that I almost got kicked out of college. Fortunately, my teacher was kind and backed me up. Being a top student and also only 15 years old certainly helped.

I did not spend much time studying. Most of my time was spent in the reading room gobbling up magazines. The outside world became more colorful and vivid. I saw pictures of fancy cars, skyscrapers, tourist attractions, and pretty girls. I read about America where people can vote and live wherever they want. They had color TVs and owned cars and houses. It was a totally different world.

Soon enough, I was in my Junior year. My classmates started worrying about where to go after graduation. Back then, the government assigned jobs to college graduates. We were numbers in the government's five-year plan. The general rule is that you go back to the province you came from unless the government needs you somewhere else.

I was homesick and looking forwards to going back home. But my college wanted me to stay as a teacher because I had the highest GPA in my class. It was considered a high honor. But I just wanted to go home. I missed home cooking and my mom. Now I was trapped again.

The only way out was to go to a graduate school. I spent a whole summer preparing for the entrance exams. I applied to Chongqing University, which was one of the best universities in my province, and hoped for the best.

To my surprise, not only I was accepted to the graduate program, but the university selected me to study in Canada. It was a miracle. I did not apply for the study abroad program. I did not think I was good enough for that. But the students who applied for that program did not do well in their English exam. I was chosen as a replacement.

Once I was in Canada, I breathed freedom. I had access to any book and any newspaper. I could express my true feelings without fear of persecution. I wanted China to be like that. It became clear that my own government lied to us. Many things I learned in high school and college were fabricated to fit its propaganda.

On June 4th, 1989, the Chinese government sent in tanks and soldiers with machine guns to the Tiananmen Square and crushed the peaceful student protest. The students wanted freedom and democracy. My wife and I supported them from Canada. We organized our fellow students in Vancouver to collect donations so we could send in tents and other materials. After the crackdown, I was blacklisted and could not go back home until both my wife and I became Canadian citizens.

After 11 years in Canada, I found a job in Indianapolis. My wife and I built our first home in Greenwood, Indiana, and raised two children. Both of them now are in college. We live a comfortable middle-class lifestyle. (You don't need much to live comfortably in Indiana.) If you ever run into someone from China or India, the chances are what got them here is Math.

WHY AND HOW I BECAME A HIGH SCHOOL MATH TEACHER

Finding My Mission and Purpose in Life

I never had a teacher who inspired me. I did not like elementary nor middle school because I was often bullied. During my 8th grade, a colleague of my dad showed me some math problems which caught my curiosity. In order to solve those problems, I taught myself algebra. So being a teacher was never in my career agenda.

But things changed in 2011. A couple of years earlier, I felt God's calling to be a high school math teacher. I gave my life to Christ in December 1996 and had led a small Chinese church since 1999, so I knew better not to run away from His calling. But I did bargain with Him. Both of my kids were still in elementary school and middle school respectively. I was the only bread earner. My daughter was in a pre-professional ballet school which was expensive for us. Teachers make not much money. So I told God that I will do it once my kids have done their colleges. I thought it is a reasonable excuse.

Of course, God did not agree with my plan. In the summer of 2010, I had a serious episode of depression. I had suffered from depression since teenage years but did not know what it is. I was diagnosed as such in July 2010. After a month of resting and taking some anti-depressant medication, I was able to go back to work. I started to feel well and a couple of months later even elated. I was having fun and worked really hard. Then everything crashed down in November and I was in another deep depression again. That is when I was diagnosed as bipolar.

In March 2011, I was let go. I suspected that it had something to do with my carelessness during my high phase. But I still felt being abandoned by my friends since I had worked with the company for 16 years. I realized a few months later that God was behind all of this.

When I started looking for jobs in that summer, I knew I had to be a high school math teacher. But I did not have a teacher's license. The best option seemed to me is to enroll in the Indianapolis Teacher Fellows program. They give a scholarship but you have to teach in an inner-city public school for a couple of years after graduation. But the application deadline was passed already for that year.

Soon it was September, and I figured I just had to wait for the next year. Then I attended a meeting of CCG (Community Church of Greenwood) daughter church pastors hosted by Dr. Charles Lake, who was the former senior pastor of CCG. After the meeting, he asked about my plan and then suggested me to try Greenwood Christian Academy (GCA). Just to show my respect, I sent in my resume. A couple of days later I had an interview with then headmaster Bruce Peters, and a couple of days later I was hired.

What happened is that the previous Calculus teacher was going to give birth and decided to stay at home. So GCA was looking for someone who can teach Calculus. Since I have a Ph.D. degree in Engineering, Mr. Peters thought I was qualified. Since GCA is a private school, he could hire a teacher without a teaching license.

So I became a high school math teacher just as God wanted. But financially I was in trouble. My starting salary was $35K, which is about one-third of what I used to make. My wife had looked for a teaching job during the summer with no avail. She is a very gifted teacher and always wanted to teach. But somehow God has never opened a door for her.

Then in November, our insurance agent called her and offered her a partnership. She first turned that offer down. But the agent persisted and eventually convinced her to work with him. So now with both of us working, we had enough to live a middle-class lifestyle (in Indiana of course).

When I first told my wife that I planned to be a high school math teacher, she said I was crazy and would not survive a year. My daughter also did not think it is a good idea. I didn't have the gifts of a teacher; I had to work hard to acquire them.

I am grateful that God pushed me out to be a teacher. I

have enjoyed my time with so many students. I felt the satisfaction of inspiring some of them to be more than they think. I experienced God's working in their lives. I looked forward to the Mondays. Above all, I have learned the lesson of trusting Him instead of my ability and circumstance.

RESCUE OUR KIDS

Breaking the School to Prison Pipeline

Our education system has been in crisis since the 80's when the famous report *A Nation at Risk* was published. It was put on life support ever since with almost one trillion dollars pouring in every year. Every administration, Clinton, Bush, and Obama, tried to revitalize it, only to make it worse in spite of good intentions and hard work by teachers and educators.

It is like a slowly sinking ship and everyone was trying to keep it afloat. After having taught in a private Christian college prep school for the past seven years, I have come to the realization that we have to abandon the ship and rescue all the people on board, particularly the students and the teachers.

Like many teachers and educators, I have tried to reform the education system within. A couple of months ago, I finally discovered its fundamental flaw. That is, no one (teachers, administrators, school boards, and government agencies) in the system has a stake in the success of the students. Naturally, the system is going to break.

The performance of a school is measured by graduation rate. So its administration is inclined to inflate the grades. Even though some teachers may resist the pressure from above, eventually they will give in and lower their standards. Today's B is F of 20 years ago. An A now could be anywhere between D, C, B, and A back then.

For teachers, it is tempting to give easy A's and B's just to keep students happy and parents off their back. In my seven years of teaching, I have not met one parent who asked me if his or her child understood what's being taught. (They thought everything was fine with their children since they got A's and B's.) Students will complain and fight for just one point for hours, but not spend a few minutes to understand a concept. Both students and their parents don't think something is wrong when the students forget everything they have learned in last school year.

So now a majority of students graduate from high schools with A's and B's. But when they get to colleges, a lot of them will find that they have to take remedial classes. Some of them will eventually drop out of college. But that will not be counted against their high schools.

Now we start to see many negative social impacts of our failed education system. Many high school graduates cannot be trained and many college graduates cannot find jobs that require a college education. Without the hope of a better future, many young people resort to drugs and alcohol.

But what can we do as an individual?

My idea is to build a global network of community based small learning academies. The smallest unit consists of a teacher and a dozen kids. It is operated as a private school owned by the teacher. This way, the success of the teacher is tied to that of the students. The teacher can raise tuition if the students are successful. Free market competition will drive out teachers who are not qualified to run a good school. So there is no need to have a teaching license.

Let us say the tuition is $500 per student per month. With 12 students, that is $6K in total. Since the academy is based in a church or a community center, the operation cost should be less than $2K. So the teacher can make over $4K per month. That is reasonable for a teacher living in Indiana.

Each academy is unique based on the teacher's experience and teaching style. One can be a coding academy, the other can be an art academy or a STEM academy. It can be for youth or grow-ups, or any other age groups.

Each teacher has access to learning resources on the network. Students learn mostly online individually. The teacher guides each student on where or from whom to learn a particular subject. There is no control over the teachers. They are free to join or leave the network.

I am sure there are many details to be worked out. But based on my thirty-eight years of combined experiences as an academic researcher, a senior engineer, an engineering manager, and a high school Math teacher, I do believe that the solution I have proposed above has a good chance to succeed.

The ship is sinking. We need to rescue the kids now. Let us work together as a team. If you are interested in becoming a teacher/owner or supporting our effort, please contact me.

FAITH, MATH, MENTAL HEALTH

Our Children Are in Danger

I felt a calling to run for school board several years ago, but I always had excuses. This year I ran out of them. This election is the final push for me to stick my neck out. This is the first time in our nation's political history that the candidates from both parties are disliked by the majority of voters. You don't want them to be your friends and certainly don't want to hire them to work for you. Yet, we are going to entrust them with our and our children's future.

How did we get here? We fell for the demagoguery and fear mongering. We were attracted to angry voices and personal attacks. We let the media tell us what is true and how we should think and vote. We had no standards of our own to judge if they are qualified. We were fooled by the simplest logic falla-cies. We don't know how to think and reason critic-

DR. PINGNAN SHI PH.D.

ally. We are quick to join sides for a shouting match.

But these are symptoms. They point to the root cause: the failure of our public education system. We had never been taught how to think and reason. We were indoctrinated and taught to follow orders, remember what were handed to us, and just pass the tests. We memorized everything yet understood nothing. As my son said, once you get to high school, you have learned not to ask whys. To cure the symptoms, we have to fix the cause.

That is why I have decided to run for school board for the Center Grove Community School Corporation. This is a well-to-do school district, yet our children do not get the education they deserve. When my son was a sophomore, his counselor told us his teachers could not teach him anymore because he knew more about Math and Science than them. He was bored and did not want to do homework since it meant nothing but getting a good grade. When my daughter graduated from middle school, we decided to put her in a Christian school for her high school education because of the drug problems and liberal propaganda.

I have heard from other parents that their Christian faith is looked down, their children's teachers don't know what they teach. The kids are frustrated with Math and cannot get help from their teachers. They were told to just remember how to do the problems so as to pass the tests.

As a father with two kids who went through Center Grove School System, I care about our next generation and fear that they are not prepared for the changing job market. Most high school graduates don't know how to learn new skills and have no math skills that are necessary to understand new technologies. You may have heard of the horror stories that some high school graduates don't know how to read and write. But the truth is most of high school graduates are math illiterate.

After much thinking, I have decided to run on the following three topics I care the most. They are Faith, Math, and Mental Health.

Faith

I grew up in Mao's China. I was raised as a communist and an atheist. Both of my parents were communists and fought for the "New China". After Mao's death, it became clear that the government lied to me through the media. Mao did not practice communism. He was a cruel dictator and starved millions of peasants to death who were supposedly the new masters of the new China. Despite of my father's wish for me to join the communist party, I abandoned communism and became a liberal (in the classic sense). I decided then I can only trust Science.

It took me much longer to finish the journey from an atheist to a Christian. My Ph.D. education and Bible study helped tremendously. I learned that Science also requires Faith. There are so many things scientists do not understand and many scientific theories are just a little better than hypothesis. As scientists, we cannot even say what is the truth. We can only say our scientific models fit the available data. I learned that Christianity is not anti-science. Instead, Christianity laid the sound logic foundation and built the social infrastructure for Science to thrive. It is no wonder almost all scientific breakthroughs were made in the West. There are more evidences for the existence of God than otherwise.

But what is more important is how my life was changed. Before I accepted Christ, my life was empty, purposeless, and meaningless. My faith gives me a direction, a purpose, and a passion to love and serve my community.

Today's young people face an uncertain future. Many of them live in broken families. Every day, they are bombarded by the media with half-truth, lies, and political propaganda. They are confused and fearful. They need a firm foundation of faith to anchor them in the stormy sea of life.

The school should make students of faith feel welcomed and embraced. It should respect their parents' faith instead of sabotaging it. Students should feel comfortable to pray for each other. Teachers should be able to pray for and with their students.

Both the DNC and RNC conventions started with a prayer. Our Congress starts its session with prayer. There are chaplains in our armed forces. There is "In God We Trust" in our currency. We have "one nation under God" in our pledge. Does it make sense in the young minds that they have to leave God outside when they step into the school entrance?

Math

We have a crisis. Most high school graduates are not equipped with sufficient math skills to succeed in college and later at work. Almost all of them do not understand algebra and calculus. The eight years of secondary math education are wasted. It may be OK for our generation, but not for theirs.

They are living in the age of rapid technology advancement. New technologies come and go. Most of jobs as we know will be replaced by industrial automation and robots. Don't believe the candidates' promise to bring manufacturing jobs back. They won't come back. The manufacturing companies may come back, but not with jobs. Those jobs will be performed by robots. Even China is now building so-called worker-less factories. Most careers that have the growth potential are in STEM fields. To thrive in this new age, math skills are essential.

Yet, our schools are not doing a good job to teach our kids math. Math teachers are either not qualified, not equipped, or simply overwhelmed. Our textbooks are outdated. State standards are not written with students in mind. They look good on paper, but fail miserably in practice.

We need to make sure that our kids are taught by qualified math teachers and in the right way. They need to learn critical problem solving skills instead of memorizing formulas and counting techniques. We need to make sure the textbooks make sense to our kids according to their mental development stages.

Mental Health

Mental illness is an epidemic. One in eight adolescents have clinical depression. 21% of children 9 to 17 years old have a diagnosable mental or addictive disorder. More teenagers and young adults die from suicide than from cancer, heart disease, AIDS, birth defects, stroke, pneumonia, influenza and chronic lung disease combined. Yet we don't talk about it. Many kids suffering from mental illness don't even talk to their parents.

Our children live in a different world. Their future is uncertain. They may not get a good job even after college. What they learn from school may become obsolete before they can use them. They eat a lot of junk food and consume a lot of salt and sugar. School lunches do not help either. Their chance of having mental illness is far greater than us.

We need to create an environment in schools for students to talk freely about mental health. They should have resources to help them understand and deal with mental illness. Mental health is as important as physical health. Our schools need to treat it with the same kind of urgency and care.

Conclusion

Dear parents, our responsibility to raise our children does not go away when we send them to school. We are held accountable for their physical, mental, and spiritual wellbeing by the same God who create us and them. I am concerned about their education, and afraid that if we as parents don't do something now, they are set up for failure when they leave us. This is why I decided to run for the school board. Please vote for me and join me for the sake of your children's education and future.

A TEACHER'S THOUGHTS ON WHAT THE FUTURE IPS SUPERINTEND- ENT SHOULD DO

Let Teachers Teach and Students Learn

IPS (Indianapolis Public Schools) now has another shot at making it a true place of learning so that inner-city students can have skills they need to be successful in the real world and become leaders in their communities. I hope a right superintendent can be found this time who will make necessary changes to transform the currently failing system.

As a teacher who has witnessed the tragedy that many students were not prepared for the real world, I'd like to share my thoughts on what we should look for in the candidates.

Focus on students' life success

Currently, we teachers teach so our students can pass standardized tests. Almost all of us don't want to do so but are forced to, because we are evaluated based on the test scores. I have taught in a private college prep school for 7 years. It boasts on graduation rate and college enrollment rate. But how many of these graduates actually finish college, we have not been told. I only know about one graduating class. After a year, 25% of them dropped out of college. How many of our graduates did well in college and later in life is unknown. No one in the school ever mentioned it.

When I started teaching, I was shocked to find out almost all of my students forgot what they learned in the past. I taught Calculus. My students were the brightest of the graduating class. They had spent the previous five years learning Pre-Algebra, Algebra I, Geometry, Algebra II, and Pre-Calc. But they had no understanding of Algebra nor Geometry. Eventually, I had to take two months to reteach them so they are able to understand Calculus.

This is also true in other subjects. For example, many of my students had learned three years of Spanish but still could not carry a conversation. A majority of our high school graduates forgot virtually everything they had learned in high school. But they did not care. Their parents were not concerned. And their teachers were not concerned either. This bothered me deeply. If they learn nothing, why should we waste our time and theirs? Why could not they use those years to learn some marketable skills?

We have to realize the reality that today's high school students learn nothing. They just memorize long enough to pass the tests. They don't have the basic skills to succeed in life. We need to change the way we educate them.

Treat teachers as professionals

We teachers are told that we are professionals, yet in reality, we are treated like assembly line workers. We are disposable and replaceable. The administration does not really care if the quality of education suffers when experienced teachers leave.

Teaching is an art. Then why we are forced to teach in a certain way? My previous principle told us that her job is to teach teachers. She has no high school teaching experience and is terrible at math. Yet she wanted me to teach in her way when one of my students complained about my teaching (I did not want to spoon feed him and he was not even trying to learn). I know many educators left education because they could not really teach.

Administrators are there to serve teachers

Administrators have too much power over teachers. They decide whether or not to extend our contracts. They may not give us a good reference when we are looking for another teaching job. People, especially parents, in general, trust them more than us because they are our bosses.

So we have to please our principles. Many times, we just simply give in to their demands. The whole school environment is optimized for their convenience and personal benefits. They can mess up our schools, and then move on to a different one.

But real education is about the students and the teachers who nurture them. Teachers should be provided with tools and other resources so they can focus on the intellectual and mental development of those under their care. A good administrator should not be the boss. He or she should serve the teachers under their care.

There are my main thoughts. I truly hope they can spark some real conversations among teachers, parents, community leaders, and legislators. We have a national education crisis. If we keep the status quo, our children will continue to suffer, and our country will suffer as a result.

REAL EDUCATION FOR INNER-CITY YOUTH

Give Them Real Education to Get Out Generational Poverty

D uring the seven years when I taught in a private Christian K-12 school, I became more and more concerned about my students' future. We may do a good job preparing them for colleges, but will they be successful afterward? I kept hearing stories about many recent college graduates who cannot find jobs worthy of a four-year college education. With a huge amount of student loan debt, it is very hard for them to achieve financial independence.

What went wrong? As I was trying to find the answer, Bill Gates' speech at the 2005 National Education Summit on High Schools opened my eyes. In front of a multitude of state governors, superintendents, and educators, he declared that "America's high schools are obsolete." However, I was not even aware of this until 2015. So far, I have not met any teacher or administrator who is aware of this speech.

Mr. Gates went so far as to say: "Until we design them (high schools) to meet the needs of the 21st century, we will keep limiting - even ruining - the lives of millions of Americans every year." A shocking statement. But it seems none in the audience was shocked enough to do anything substantial afterward.

America's high school education was designed in the 1870's to prepare students for higher education. But over the years, the standard for high school graduation has been lowered so much that most of high school graduates are not ready for college. This is especially true in inner cities and small towns. Without the hope to ever go to colleges, 4-year high school education became a huge waste of time and taxpayers' money. But the real tragedy is that those students who give up going to college are easily lured into gangs, drugs, and sex trafficking.

For too long, we were hoping our governments will do something while millions of youth ended up in prisons, on streets, in graves, or died of drug overdose. We, as citizens and parents, have to take the responsibility now. As a Christian, I know I have to give an account when my time on earth is up.

That is why I have started a truly innovative high school near Indianapolis' Fountain Square. The objective is to transform inner-city high school students into successful entrepreneurs. Teaching them the entrepreneur mindset that you are responsible for your future, don't wait for handouts, and go make things happen. I also want to empower them with skills and knowledge to get out of generational poverty and revitalize their communities.

My school is called Poema Entrepreneurship Academy. Poema is a Latin word from which English word Poem came. To me, every student is a poem to be written by God. As a teacher, I am there to be His hand and experience His working. Poema itself came from the Greek word Poiema which was used in Ephesians 2:10 as God's workmanship. Each and every child is precious to Him!

In my school, students spend a half day working as apprentices in the local businesses and take classes in the other half. There are only five core subjects: Biblical foundation, language, Math, entrepreneurship, and computer technology. They will be worth at least 20 high school credits. Students are encouraged to take other subjects of their interests as self-studies. They only need to study for 2 years to graduate.

Students are responsible for a $500 per month tuition. Their parents are not allowed to pay for them. This is to teach them the mindset that it is their education, their future, and hence their responsibility. They will learn how to raise fund, find sponsors, start and run a business.

When they graduate with a high school equivalency diploma, they have all the options available. They can keep run and scale up their businesses, go to a traditional trade school, or a coding academy. If they decide to go to college, they can go to a two-year college prep program where they will take AP and dual credit courses.

I want to rescue inner-city kids from the school to prison pipeline and give them real hope and a good future. We cannot count on the politicians and the obsolete education system. Please join me in this mission. In a rich and free country like ours, it is a shame to let millions of kids be locked up and abandoned in poverty. We send money to help kids in other countries, why don't we do something for the kids in our own cities?

HIGH SCHOOL EDUCATION SHOULD BE OPTIONAL

Not Everyone Needs College Education, So Why Waste Time and Money Preparing for It?

America's high school education system is oriented toward preparing students for college. However, in 2020, only 62.7% of high school graduates enrolled in college. Nearly 60% of them need to take remedial courses. This means only about 25% of high school graduates are ready for college. It also means that high school education is a waste of time for three out of four high school graduates, at the cost of 100 billion dollars per year for taxpayers.

What went wrong?

For starters, many decades ago, students had to pass meaningful entrance exams to get into high schools, which ensured that the incoming students were ready for rigorous high school education. Back then, you might have to take classical Greek and Latin. Students who weren't admitted chose to work or learn a trade instead.

Now students can get into public high schools without assessment. The majority of them are not ready. This makes preparing those students for college an uphill battle for high school teachers. Most of them simply give up.

Secondly, high school administrators allow students to move to a higher grade even when they don't pass standardized assessments. For example, in 2020, Indiana's high school graduation rate was about 87%. A year earlier, only one-third of the same student body had passed ISTEP, Indiana's standardized test. (High school ISTEP only tests on contents up to the 10th grade.)

What does this mean? Unless the students had upped their game or the schools had done something magical, about 62% of those high school graduates did not pass the ISTEP test. Another data point to consider is a study done in 2019 that shows the average college freshman reads at the 7th-grade level.

And so, a proverbial can is being kicked from elementary schools to middle schools to high schools to colleges. Another study shows that more than 50% of students attending two-year colleges must take remedial classes, and about one-third of students attending four-year colleges are required to take remedial courses. Those are classes they had already taken in high school. Now they have to retake them at the cost of college tuition, and many of them do not go on to graduate from college.

Let us also consider the financial cost of this. A report from the Center for American Progress in 2016 finds that remedial education costs students and their families about $1.3 billion annually. They paid a huge financial price for the failure of high school education. Furthermore, about 40% of the students enrolled in remedial courses at two-year colleges never finish them.

The third cause is the lack of competent and caring teachers, especially high school math teachers. The documentary *Waiting for Superman* presented how the largest teachers' union, the National Education Association (NEA), protected incompetent and even mean-spirited teachers. A teacher can get tenure in just three years. Once they get it, it is a difficult, expensive, and lengthy process for administrators to fire them.

This puts new teachers in a difficult situation. An article in January 2020 on the website of The National Association of Secondary School Principals reported that nearly half of new teachers in the first five years quit, and one-third of them leave the profession altogether. New teachers are often vulnerable targets of mistreatment.

Another article on ToughNickel claims:

> *"The main reasons teachers walk away from their*

jobs is because of the poor working conditions, unreasonable demands, and unrealistic expectations they face every day. Collectively, these factors make the teaching profession unbearable for even the best educators."

One reason for the lack of competent high school math teachers is the NEA's insistence that all teachers should be compensated equally. But the market value of someone good at math is very different from that of someone who teaches social studies. Competent math teachers can easily find other jobs that pay two, three, even four times their teaching salary.

I propose this solution:

Make high school education optional. Make sure only the students who are ready for high school get into high school. And make certain only competent teachers teach them. Meanwhile, make high school level trade schools as widely available and accessible as high schools currently are.

Not everyone needs to go to college. There are many other good options. In many other countries, students will go to trade schools if they don't want to or cannot go to college. But in America, parents have been conditioned to send their children to college no matter what. Now we have a shortage of plumbers, electricians, carpenters, and other trade professionals. Check out these 24 highest-paying trade jobs. They are all above $50K (median salary). How many college graduates nowadays can make that kind of money?

Terrell Clemons wrote about "credential

inflation" in *Salvo* 51. Now a bachelor's degree is not good enough; you have to borrow more money to get a master's degree. The millennials and their parents are facing the disheartening reality of "a glut of graduates with a high debt/low employability imbalance."

But I doubt that politicians will take this one. The NEA is too powerful for them. Fortunately, American parents have the choice. They can help their children decide if going to college is a good investment. They can encourage their children to consider trade schools.

Things will change when American parents realize that their children are not prepared for the real world and blindly sending them to college may make them lifelong slaves of the student loan industry. I am hopeful that when enough parents decide to take action, we can force our elected officials to make the long-overdue change.

* This article was first published in Salvo.

THE RESPONSE OF A CHINESE AMERICAN EDUCATOR TO IBRAM X. KENDI'S *HOW TO BE AN ANTIRACIST*

A New Variant of Marxism Is Spreading In America

Ideologies matter. I should know. I am a survivor of Communism: an ideology that has murdered more than 100 million and enslaved more than 1 billion people around the world.

Ideologies are mostly formulated, refined, remixed, and taught by professors in colleges and universities. In general, these professors are scholarly, kind, and respected by their students and colleagues. However, how their ideologies eventually flow to the society and influence policies and policymakers is beyond their control.

When Karl Marx was formulating his ideology, he could not foresee the horrible consequences of its application. He saw the horrific social inequality in Europe at the time and proposed a vision of a new world where everyone is equal. His means was through a socialist revolution in capitalist countries.

But Lenin and Mao both took his ideas one step further. The former believed that it could happen in a feudalist country like Russia and the latter in an agrarian country like China. Both believed in revolution through military power. Once they took control of their respective countries, they instituted a dictatorship government instead. Mao, in fact, murdered far more Marxists than his arch-rival, Chiang Kai-shek.

So to understand the consequences of an ideology, we need to look at both its end and means. Is the end realistic and achievable? Does the means serve the end?

When I was reading Ibram X. Kendi's *How to Be an Antiracist*, I couldn't help but think about Communism. His ideology is a variant of Marxism, substituting class with race. The struggle between bourgeoisie and proletariat is replaced with the struggle between racist and antiracist. Let us call his ideology Kendiism. It is useful to put a name to it; because there are many people in universities, mainstream media, the entertainment industry, and public education system who have openly embraced this ideology.

Let us examine its end first. Kendiism wants to achieve a world of racial equity. Kendi didn't define racial equity explicitly, but by the examples he gave for racial inequity, we can deduce that it is a society where everything is in proportional representation to the racial make-up in the total population.

For example, the latest update from the Federal Bureau of Prisons shows these percentages of inmates by race: whites 57.8%, blacks 38.4%, and Asians 1.5%. Compare this to the percentages in the general population as of 2019: whites 60.1%, blacks 12.2%, and Asians 5.6%. In Kendiism, this is the definite evidence of systematic and structural racism because the black prisoner percentage is more than three times that of the general population.

Of course, equity applies to every aspect of life in Kendiism's ideal world. There should likewise be a proportional number of black CEOs, black teachers, black politicians, black college students, etc. But how can you make this happen?

Kendiism's means is through racial discrimination. Kendi wrote:

> *"The only remedy to racist discrimination is antiracist discrimination. The only remedy to past discrimination is present discrimination. The only remedy to present discrimination is future discrimination."*

What does that mean? Take the aforementioned prison population, for example. The Asian prisoner percentage is only 1.5%. But Asians in the general population count for 5.6%. Should the court give a harsher sentence to Asians? To Kendiism, justice is not blind.

Does this sound far-fetched? But similar things have already happened.

In 2014, the organization Students for Fair Admissions sued Harvard claiming that the college discriminates against Asian-American applicants in its undergraduate admissions process.

Here is an excerpt from Wikipedia:

> *"Peter Arcidiacono, a Duke economist testifying on behalf of the plaintiffs, concluded that Asian-American applicants as a group performed stronger on objective measures of academic achievement and extracurricular activities. Despite this, they received a statistically significant penalty relative to white applicants in the personal score and overall score assigned by Harvard officials. As a result, Asian-American applicants have the lowest chance of admission of all racial groups in the United States despite scoring highest in all objective measurements."*

In 2018, among the admitted students to Harvard, the average SAT score of Asian Americans was 766.6 while for African Americans it was 703.7. Harvard has a racist policy against Asian Americans in the name of racial diversity and equity.

In May 2021, the University of California announced that it would no longer take SAT/ACT scores into consideration for admission. This policy allows the university to play number games to achieve perceived "racial equity" at the expense of hardworking students.

Kendi's parents' generation believes that African Americans have to work harder to catch up. They recognize that past injustices damaged black family and community structures. The absence of fathers in black families makes social upward mobility much harder. They have worked hard to build up families and communities in the hope of achieving Dr. King's dream, where his "four little children will one day live in a nation where they will not be judged by the color of their skin but by the content of their character."

But to Kendiism, color-blindness is racist. Dr. King was a racist because he wanted a color-blind America. Kendiism asserts that there are no problems in African American communities as if the past racial injustices had not done any damage. It claims that the perceived inequality is solely the result of policies. Therefore, to achieve an equitable society, the only means is through policies and policymakers.

This leads us back to Communism. Both of my parents were communists. They believed in the future of a just and equal society. But just like other communist countries, the means to achieve that dream created a hell on earth.

History teaches us that if you give a government the power to do good, it will inevitably misuse it to do harm.

Lord Acton wrote his famous line in a letter: "Power tends to corrupt, and absolute power corrupts absolutely. Great men are almost always bad men."

Two frequently used words in How to Be an Antiracist are "race" and "power". Kendiism wants power to bring racial equity. That kind of power would affect every aspect of people's lives. The kind of government it would inevitably produce is totalitarian.

As a matter of fact, Kendi himself made it very clear:

> *"Capitalism is essentially racist; racism is essentially capitalist. They were birthed together from the same unnatural causes, and they shall one day die together from unnatural causes."*

He proposed to establish a Department of Anti-racism (DOA) staffed by antiracist experts like himself that:

> *"... would be responsible for preclearing all local, state and federal public policies to ensure they won't yield racial inequity, monitor those policies, investigate private racist policies when racial inequity surfaces, and monitor public officials for expressions of racist ideas. The DOA would be empowered with disciplinary tools to wield over and against policymakers and public officials who do not voluntarily change their racist policy and ideas."*

Have we ever had such an agency with this kind of power in America? Never! But there were such agencies in Nazi Germany and the Soviet Union. There are still such agencies in Communist China and North Korea.

Kendiism promises a future of racial equity, but its means would create a totalitarian government. It is not what Kendi wants. But if history is a guide, we can see the inevitable end. Kendiism is neo-Marxism.

If you think Kendiism is radical, consider this: *How to Be an Antiracist* is a recommended reading for teens and adults in many, possibly all, of America's school districts. I urge you to read it and see what kind of harm and danger to our republic Kendiism will inflict through our public education system funded by our tax dollars.

AN OPEN LETTER TO PUBLIC SCHOOL PARENTS

It Is High Time to Take Back Education

Dear parents:

We have entrusted our children to the school board to give them a high-quality education so they can be successful in life. However, that trust has been betrayed.

Currently, Critical Race Theory (CRT) is not taught as a subject; but as an ideology, it is permeated in every subject. For example, many school districts recommend books by authors such as Ibram X. Kendi's *Antiracist*

Baby for younger readers (ages 3 to 7) and *How to Be an Antiracist* for teens and parents.

Kendi asserts that America is a racist country. In his book, *How to Be an Antiracist*, he never gives any example of current policies. The racist policies he quotes are all before the Civil Rights movement. To him, the statistics that show disproportionally blacks in poverty and prison are good enough to accuse America of having systemic, structural, and institutional racism.

His solution is through racial discrimination. Dr. King wanted a color-blind society, but color-blindness is racist to Kendi. His hero is Malcolm X, who was a militant black supremacist. He wants our children to be "racially conscious" and to view the world through the lens of race struggle.

Kendi divided Americans into racists and anti-racists. If you don't support his brand of anti-racism, you are by definition a racist. To him, an anti-racist is necessarily an anti-capitalist. He wants to build a so-called equitable society, a Utopia where every race is proportionally represented in every aspect of life. This is Marxism in a different branding.

Unfortunately, many teachers are already indoctrinated in college by their professors to convert their students into social activists. Some of them are zealous social justice warriors who signed a pledge to teach CRT in their classrooms even if it is banned.

Just recently the biggest teachers union, National Education Association (NEA) passed a resolution to push CRT onto K-12 public schools in spite of overwhelming opposition from parents. School board members need to make a public stand on whether or not they oppose the NEA's decision.

CRT ideology has already been sneaked in under Social-Emotional Learning (SEL). As a matter of fact, Karen Niemi, the president and CEO of CASEL which is dedicated to making SEL an integral part of K-12 education, openly declared that "social-emotional learning must actively contribute to anti-racism ... we see SEL as a tool for anti-racism." Their goal is to turn our children into so-called anti-racists.

We want our children to have the best education available so they can have a better future. But NEA and many teachers have a different agenda. They want to use our children as pawns to fundamentally change America. We have to hold school board members accountable for safeguarding our children against neo-Marxist indoctrination.

Please take action before they ruin your children.

AMERICA'S PUBLIC EDUCATION VS. CHINA'S STATE RUN EDUCATION

Are They Working Together to Destroy America?

When my son started first grade, his language and math skills were at the third-grade level, thanks to his private kindergarten. So, he was extremely bored at school. When we asked him what he learned, he always replied: "The same thing: one, two, three, and ABC." When my wife asked his school to give him something at his level, they told her there was no such accommodation. As a result, my son learned nothing from his school for the first three years. Worse, he developed a habit of not paying attention in class.

Many Asian, especially Chinese, parents are puzzled by America's education philosophy that is more concerned about students' mental well-being than academic competence. In China, there are top-notch kindergartens, elementary, middle, and high schools. You have to pass highly competitive exams to get into them. Their education system caters to the talented and hard-working students to produce the best scientists and engineers.

Habi Zhang, a young mother and doctoral student studying political science in the U.S., was dismayed to find out her son had little homework in America. In her opinion piece in the Wall Street Journal on November 21, 2021, she wrote:

> *Hattie had recently finished two years of elementary school in Chengdu, China, where he trotted off to school each day with a backpack stuffed with thick textbooks and materials for practices and quizzes. Here he leaves for school with little in his backpack other than a required "healthy snack."*

But her concern is what this means to the future of America. Like many freedom-loving Chinese, she is worried about China's goal to overtake America as the number one global power. She asks:

> *How will America compete with a China determined to train the best mathematicians, scientists and engineers?*

She has also realized that America is going through a cultural revolution:

> *Unfolding now are two Maoist cultural revolutions, one in the East and the other in the West. The former is a jingoistic nationalism enforced by party loyalties and ubiquitous secret police. The latter is an anti-Americanism enforced by progressive mobs seeking to defund the police. Both are about limiting expression, controlling thought and regulating behavior.*

The difference in the two education systems is alarming:

> *Chinese education pushes the young in directions that serve the party and the state. Youth are trained to be skilled laborers ready to endure hard work and brutal competition. Such political indoctrination is taught side by side with math and science. American education is supposed to be about opening minds but appears not to fill them with much. Worse, young Americans are not prepared for the demands of being an adult.*

When I started my teaching career in 2011 after retiring from engineering, I was shocked at how much coddling American students had. I taught at a private college prep school. The first math quiz I gave was not challenging and could be completed during a regular class. Yet, a significant percentage of students didn't finish it and asked for an extension.

I wanted to teach them a life lesson to work harder and be more disciplined going forward. But they complained to the headmaster, and I had to give them another class time to finish the quiz at the cost of the majority of students who had completed it.

More and more American parents have realized that there is not much learning going on in schools. But is this the result of failure, or is it intended by design?

Ms. Zhang notices that America's higher education has changed for the worse:

> *This phenomenon started in higher education. For years attending American universities, I have been disturbed to watch colleges fabricate "anxiety" and "depression" in students who are not mentally ill. Administrators have used grossly exaggerated terms such as "trauma," and melodramatic expressions such as "I cannot begin to imagine what you have suffered," to turn into a catastrophe what is best described as disappointment. This creates a culture of victimization.*

As a victim of and an eyewitness to China's Cultural Revolution, I appreciate Ms. Zhang for her effort to wake up the American people. We do have a determined enemy without, and we may also have an enemy within. Both are working toward the destruction of America and the Western Civilization.

* This article was first published in Salvo.

THE UNDECLARED CULTURAL REVOLUTION IN AMERICA

*What We Can Learn From
China's Cultural Revolution*

We are already in a cultural revolution in America. It was never officially declared and took decades to prepare. But the end result is that now the main culture is neo-Marxist, with Christianity having receded to a counterculture. To understand this cultural revolution, it helps to take a history lesson from the infamous Cultural Revolution in China from 1966 to 1976.

I was three when it began, so most of my formative years coincided with it. Almost overnight, everything was turned upside down. What used to be good is now bad; what used to be bad is now good.

Intellectuals used to be regarded highly and now are considered lower than prostitutes. Peasants and workers are now the ruling class (in reality only Mao was the real master).

Almost every book was banned. All the adults and school-age kids, especially those from the so-called bourgeoisie class (middle and upper-middle classes), had to undergo re-education trainings to "wash away" the bad influences from the past.

Intellectuals were rounded up and put in labor camps. All the key positions were filled with Mao's loyalists. K-12 schools, colleges, and universities were all closed. (K-12 schools were reopened in 1970, and some colleges were reopened in 1973.)

Religion was banned. Temples and churches were closed or demolished. Christians, Buddhists, and Taoists were sent to labor camps if they didn't renounce their faith. Buddhist priests were forced to get married. Bibles were banned and burned.

Almost all movies and theater performances were banned. During the 10 years of the Cultural Revolution, only eight so-called model dramas and their variants were performed. All books published before the revolution were banned and a great many of them were also destroyed.

History was rewritten. The famous first emperor of China, Qin Shi Huang, was considered a tyrant for his brutal reign. But now he is a hero because he unified China. Confucius was revered as the greatest educator. But now he is the great accomplice because his teachings were used to maintain the status quo.

All western names were erased from textbooks because they were Western imperialists and colonists. For example, Newton's laws in physics were replaced with "law number one", "law number two", etc. All of the scientific achievements were not the results of scientists, but the hard work of members of the working class like the lab assistants and janitors.

Almost all the statues, some as old as two or three thousand years, were beheaded or toppled. Antique artifacts and artworks were destroyed or taken by the Red Guards.

Middle and high school students and college students were organized into these so-called Red Guards. They swore their allegiance to Mao and Mao alone. And he unleashed them to turn the whole country upside down. In Beijing alone, in the two months of August and September 1966, 1,772 people were beaten to death; many of them were teachers, professors, and principals. Many famous writers, artists, and musicians chose suicide to escape from further humiliation. More than thirty thousand families were ransacked.

For about a year there was pure terror all across China. The Red Guards used many forms of torture, confiscated private properties, and drove many families out of cities. Many of the victims were intellectuals who once believed that Mao and the communists would bring democracy and science to China.

After they finished with the common enemies, the Red Guards split into two factions. One was led by children of party officials and the other by children of workers and peasants. They started with big letter posts and attacked each other with words. Very soon it escalated into physical violence, and eventually to battles with real weapons. 30,000 to 50,000 red guards died from 1967 to 1968. There is a mountain in my home city that is full of the graves of teenage Red Guards.

Mao started the Cultural Revolution to seize absolute power. He used the Red Guards to dismantle the whole party apparatus and government structure. In the end, he became the god and savior of the Chinese people. His words were the highest authority. He could kill or imprison whomever he didn't like.

Once he controlled the country, he tricked the Red Guards to go to farmlands far away from cities in the name of re-education by the peasants. He said the students were educated in the old education system, therefore they needed to purge any remnants of bourgeoisie influence in their behaviors and thoughts.

Some universities were opened in 1974. But the qualification for admission was not the academic aptitude. It was your class identity and loyalty to Mao. You had to be a child of a party official, a peasant, or a worker.

In the end, Chinese traditional values and cultures were totally destroyed. Arising from the ashes emerged a brutal, absolute dictatorship. China became a police state where you could not trust anyone and dared not even to hold thoughts that were not within party lines. You constantly had to criticize yourself, your spouse, your parents, your children, and others. You would never know when the police would knock on your door and make you disappear.

This brings us back to America. We are in a cultural revolution of our own. When it started is not clear, but we can trace it as far back as the '60s when radical college students wanted to overthrow America's government. They adored Mao and wanted to bring the Cultural Revolution to America. They occupied university campuses and some, like members of the infamous Weather Underground, even bombed federal buildings.

Then it fizzled. To their surprise, the working class did not join them. They disappeared from the public view. But they did not give up their fight. Many of them such as Bill Ayers became professors.

From the '80s, popular culture started to change. Homosexuality went from a perversion to an acceptable behavior to a celebrated sexual identity. Divorce became commonplace. Sex before marriage became the norm. LGBQT + lifestyles are now taught all the way down to the kindergarten level.

The process was gradual, so the majority of Americans did not notice. But if we compare the current culture with that before the '60s, we see the result of a revolution. What used to be bad is now good. What used to be good is now bad. Christianity is now the counter-culture. Even the Western Civilization itself is demonized in academia and popular culture.

But in the last two years, American parents have started to wake up. 2020 gave them an unprecedented opportunity to see what their children were learning at schools.

They did not like it. They saw their children were confused about their gender identities. They saw teachers using made-up pronouns. They saw their children being told they were oppressors or oppressed purely based on their skin color.

The conservatives are also waking up. They saw the riots instigated or organized by groups like Antifa and BLM. They saw how the mainstream media distorted reality. They saw their state and federal governments overreach their authorities to declare emergency and close businesses.

I believe the communists overplayed their hand this time. It is the new phase of their revolution, but they started it too soon. The pushing of Critical Race Theory (CRT) onto K-12 public schools gives parents and conservatives no choice but to fight back. This neo-Marxist ideology, as declared by its proponents, aims to fundamentally dismantle the Judeo-Christian foundation on which America was built and stands. It wants to replace our capitalist economy with a totalitarian economy. It has rewritten America's history. It pits people of color, especially the blacks, to fight against the whites.

Can we still win? Right now, they have the upper hand. They control the public education system, popular culture, the media, and higher education. But we still have a chance. We have federal and state constitutions that limit the power of the federal and state governments. In many states, parents have the choice of how to educate their children. And voters can elect school board members who are for them and vote in real constitutional conservatives. But we have to act now before it is too late.

* This article was first published in Salvo.

FAITH, ACADEMICS, NO POLITICS

Will You Save Your Children and/or Grandchildren

I n 2016, I ran for the Center Grove School Board. My slogan at that time was "Faith, Math, and Mental Health." I wrote an open letter to the parents and got 3,456 votes. Not enough to win, but it gave me hope that there were enough voters who truly cared about Center Grove Community Schools.

I have decided to run for Center Grove School Board again next year. My slogan this time is "Faith, Academics, and No Politics."

Faith

At the start of every school day, students say the pledge of allegiance. One of the key phrases is "One nation, under God, indivisible." America is unique in that its founding was based on the belief that "all men are created equal, that they are endowed by their Creator with certain unalienable Rights, that among these are Life, Liberty and the pursuit of Happiness" and governments are instituted to protect these rights.

As Americans, our rights are not granted by any government. They were gifted from God. Why should we keep Him out of our public schools funded by our tax dollars?

Our public education started its long decline since prayers were taken out from public schools in 1962 by the Supreme Court - the same court once deemed slavery was legal. Before that, there were Ten Commandments plaques hanging on the walls by the principals' offices, and students started their day with the Lord's Prayers. Their absence has created a spiritual vacuum and confusion among students and allowed the invasion of Eastern religious practices and atheist and Communist ideologies.

We should give students the opportunity to learn about the history of the Christian faith and how it created the Western Civilization and influenced the founding of our Republic. They should be encouraged to seek comfort, peace, and wisdom from the Bible. Teachers should be allowed to pray for and with their students.

Today's students are living in a rapidly changing society. They face an uncertain future. Only faith can keep them grounded and secure. Years ago, the belief that God was on their side kept the patriots fighting against the mighty British army. Today, our children need that same assurance to be hopeful.

Madalyn Murray O'Hair, a die-hard atheist among others, was instrumental in the Supreme Court's ruling to ban prayers in public schools. She didn't like students in her son's class reciting the Lord's Prayer at the start of each school day. Instead of opting her son out, she embarked on a crusade to ban prayers in public schools altogether. Ironically, her son later became a Baptist minister.

O'Hair went on to file many lawsuits to remove Christianity from public life, including removing the phrase "In God We Trust" from American currency.

Think about it: an atheist denied the opportunity for public school students to express their Christian faith. Every US president so far was sworn to the office with his right hand on his personal or family Bible. The US Congress starts its sessions with prayers. Many local governments start their meetings with prayers and the pledge of allegiance. "In God We Trust" is still on American coins and bills and is still the official motto of the United States. But our children are not allowed to start their day with a prayer.

If we want to restore our schools, we have to get back to the place before we went astray.

Academics

Grade inflation is real. Today's A and B are yesterday's C and D, even F. It is well documented that most American high school graduates are not prepared for college, let alone for the real world. Parents have the right and authority to demand high academic standards. They have the right and authority to know whether or not their children get the kind of education they expect. Unfortunately, they have been misled by inflated grades.

The district average of Center Grove elementary and middle schools for 2021 ILEARN ELA and Math proficiency is 45.8%. The lowest, sadly, is Sugar Grove Elementary, where both of my children attended, at 35.4%. This is simply not acceptable. We should and can do better. The school board should be held accountable.

Parents have the right and authority to know the true state of the education of their children's schools. They need that information to decide whether or not to let their children stay, move them to a different school, or homeschool them.

We need to seriously examine the curricula and textbooks. Many textbooks were not written for the students. Math textbooks, in particular, are fragmented. Unrelated topics are mixed together. Students move from one chapter to the next without understanding the previous one. The end result is that almost all high school students hate math as a subject.

We can do better.

No Politics

During the last school year, many parents were able to see what their children were learning, and they did not like it. There was little learning but a lot of political indoctrination. It is not a secret that the Ed for Red movement was purely political.

I was alarmed in May this year by the hiring of the DEI (Diversity, Equity, and Inclusion) director at Carmel Clay Community School Corporation. It reminded me of the political officers I knew when I was in elementary school during the Cultural Revolution. Their job was to enforce party control and to indoctrinate us with Communist propaganda. We were encouraged to criticize our classmates, teachers, and even parents. We were told the meaning of our lives was to advance Communism all over the world.

I found on the Diversity page of the Center Grove Community School Corporation's website the resources for teens and parents (it was later taken down). One of the listed books was *How to Be an Antiracist* by Ibram X. Kendi. I spent a week studying that book and then wrote an essay, which is included in this book, to share my counterpoints.

I then spent a month studying Critical Race Theory (CRT) which is the ideology behind Kendi's book. Based on the theorists' books and articles, I traced its root to Marxism. It is not an obscure theory in academia as portrayed by the media. Even the theorists themselves have claimed that it is a movement to fundamentally change America. This neo-Marxism ideology has already taken over America's higher education and has permeated social sciences, media, big corporations, and Hollywood.

What we parents have witnessed in the past several months is the down push of this ideology by higher education, teachers' unions, and some foundations. Many teachers have already been indoctrinated in college and/or during professional development that their goal is to make social activists. Many were led to believe that parents have no right to influence what is taught to their children. And many believe that they are saving their students from their parents. Our public education has been hijacked by social justice warriors.

But we parents can take it back. We can protect our children from political indoctrination and hold the school board accountable. Fortunately, in this country, we still have the freedom to choose how to educate our children.

My Promises

If elected, I will first work hard to regain your trust. You had entrusted your children to the school board. You elected the board members to represent you and work for your interests. Unfortunately, that trust was betrayed. The new school board needs to work hard to regain it. I will keep open communication with concerned parents and grassroots parent organizations.

I will examine curricula and textbooks. I will sound the alarm if there is any political indoctrination or pornographic materials. I will team up with you if you want to get involved.

I will work with the administration and teachers to make sure parents have open access to what is taught to their children. Without this measure, the board cannot regain your trust. You have the right to know what your children are learning and whether or not your children are receiving a high-quality education.

I am sure there will be a lot for me to learn and there is a limit to what I can do. But I will always be honest to you and hold myself and the board accountable to you.

EDUCATION 4.0

Transforming Students to Masters Instead of Slaves

P eople have talked about Education 3.0 or 4.0. Some have even spoken about 5.0. But by software development standards, they can only be qualified as 3.x since they all are various sorts of improvements on the current education system.

Here I give a rough sketch of the first three versions of education and then describe the fourth one as clearly as possible, under the constraints of this short essay. This is definitely to be painted in very broad strokes. But hopefully, I can show you the forest without giving details of individual trees.

Education 1.0

Ever since the beginning of civilization, education has been a top priority for the ruling class to ensure that their cities, states, or kingdoms can thrive or at least survive. The objective of education was to transform a boy into a master to best manage his inheritance. This is what I call *Education 1.0*. Typically, a student was served by several teachers. For example, in ancient China, a prince had to learn literature, math, music, archery, sword fighting, painting, and chariot riding from respective masters.

Education back then was only meant for the few. The masses were kept in ignorance for the convenience of governing by the ruling class.

Education 2.0

Later on, education was extended to smart kids so they could become professionals to serve their masters, such as officials serving in royal courts. The book of Daniel in the Old Testament recorded that Daniel and his friends were handpicked to study the language and literature of the Babylonians so they could serve Nebuchadnezzar.

Students, exclusively male, were trained to be loyal and willing to die for their masters. There were private schools that teach specialized skills such as fighting, accounting, and bookkeeping. One example is the samurais in feudal Japan. This kind of education is what I call *Education 2.0*.

In this version, education was expanded to the most gifted children. But the masses were still kept uneducated.

Education 3.0

Due to the First Industrial Revolution, a massive educated workforce was needed to take on rapidly increasing blue- and white-collar jobs. Workers had to have some skill at reading, writing, and basic arithmetic. Thus public education was necessary. This is what I call *Education 3.0*. Its objective is to transform boys and girls into well-behaved servants.

Plato defined a slave as one who lives for someone else's purposes. A rich slave is nevertheless a slave. A powerful slave is still a slave. Even the CEO of a global company can be laid off and has to leave his fancy office in a few minutes with the assistance of a security guard or two. In this sense, the objective of Education 3.0, just as Education 2.0 is to train students to become educated slaves, but on a mass scale.

Because of the differences in the objectives of these three versions, the art of teaching is different. In Education 1.0, teachers are usually well experienced and successful in the real world. They wanted to pass their skills, experience, knowledge, connection, and wisdom to their students in the last chapter of their lives. Each teacher was a master in his field who taught his students to become the new ones. Each teacher has a unique style of teaching. But they all serve the same student.

In Education 2.0, students sought out their teachers. Often several of them learn together from the same teacher. The teacher is typically well experienced. One example is Confucius in ancient China. Many universities in the West during the Middle Ages were places where students could become professionals. Each professor had his own teaching style and specialty.

In Education 3.0, students were manufactured into workers. Everything is standardized. Students go from one grade to a higher one until graduation as if on a conveyor belt. They move from one classroom to another following rigidly timed schedules. They are taught by using the same textbooks and evaluated based on the same tests. They all have to fit into one standardized box. Teachers are treated as hired hands on an assembly line. They are disposable and exchangeable. Most of them have never even worked in the real world.

This version had worked for America's economy until about thirty years ago. Many students from low-income families did move up into the middle class.

However, due to the mass adoption of computer technology and the Internet, our economy has changed drastically and is still evolving. Now it no longer needs that many workers. Robots and Artificial Intelligence are replacing both blue- and white-collar workers. Unfortunately, schools have not changed and still produce graduates who are not prepared for the new economy. They are like the once giant Kodak, which had never caught up with the digital age.

In 2019, 57 million Americans (nearly 35% of the US workforce) were freelancing, and 60% of them were doing so by choice. That sector will grow in the coming years. It will be harder and harder to find a job working for a company and do the same thing until retirement. At the same time, it will become easier and easier to start small businesses. This new economy is for entrepreneurs.

However, our current education system was not designed for producing entrepreneurs and is actually detrimental to any student with an entrepreneurial spirit. Many business owners I know were considered troublemakers and rebels in high schools. They did not want to work for someone and were too free-spirited and independent to be obedient, good boys or girls. As far as the education system is concerned, they were the defects.

Education 4.0

We now need a major upgrade, a new version, if you will. We need *Education 4.0.* The objective, interestingly enough, is the same as that of Education 1.0, but on a mass scale. (Entrepreneurs, by definition, are masters of their businesses.) Any student who wants to become an entrepreneur can be educated as such. We have the means and the resources.

Here I propose a model to give some details about this new education paradigm. I envision a global network of community-based small learning academies. Each academy can be as small as one teacher and a dozen students. The teacher owns and runs the academy so that his or her self-interest is tied to the students' future success. (A fundamental flaw in Education 3.0 is that no one in the system has a stake in the future success of the students.)

Because of the availability of many subjects on the Internet, a teacher does not have to be a subject expert. His or her role is a mentor and a coach whose responsibility is to encourage and cheer their students to achieve as much as their talents permit. Each student is cultivated as an individual with different talents, temperaments, and learning styles. Each student is taught to learn on his or her own.

Each academy is a private school that is not accredited by any government entity so that the teacher has full freedom of teaching. It is community-based so that the teacher and his or her students have the community's support. As it is often said: "It takes a village to raise a child," any community has to invest in their young to have a future. Churches are well suited to provide such education to the children of their congregations.

One of such schools I have envisioned provides a two-year high school education for entrepreneurs. The students spend half the day working as apprentices in the local businesses and the other half learning. There are only five core subjects for them to study: Biblical Entrepreneurship, Practical English, Practical Math, Business IT, and Business Operation. Students are encouraged to study other subjects that they like.

After two years, they can graduate with a high school equivalency diploma and pursue further education for their vocations. They can start a business or go to a trade school. Students who want to go to higher education will be provided with two more years of college preparation, taking AP and dual credit courses. This way, instead of forcing every student to go through four years of high school education, most of them only need to spend two years learning real-life skills. Only those who really want to go to college need to study for four years.

To me, as an educator, this is exciting. Education transformed my life from a small-town boy in China to an accomplished professional in America. I believe that Education 4.0 will lift many inner-city youths out of generational poverty and revitalize their communities. It is uncharted territory with many unknowns, risks, and opportunities. As a traveler in this world, I look forward to this new adventure. I invite you to come along and help your children and grandchildren become truly free in the land of the free.

ABOUT THE AUTHOR

Pingnan Shi

 Dr. Pingnan Shi, Ph.D., aka Dr. Ping, grew up in China during the Cultural Revolution. After a successful engineering career with 15 US patents, he became a high school math teacher in 2011. During the seven years teaching in a Christian private college prep school, Dr. Ping became disillusioned but later enlightened by the late John T. Gatto, Dorothy L. Sayers, and others. In the past five years, he has written numerous essays to wake up American parents to take back their children's education. This book is a collection of some of those essays.